The Honey Bee's Hive
A Thriving City

by Joyce Markovics

Consultant: Brian V. Brown
Curator, Entomology Section
Natural History Museum of Los Angeles County

BEARPORT
PUBLISHING

New York, New York

Credits

Cover and Title Page, © Dwight Kuhn/Dwight Kuhn Photography; 4L, © Nancy Hoyt Belcher/Grant Heilman Photography; 4R, © Seleznev Valery/Shutterstock; 5T, © Milena/Shutterstock; 5B, © Phil Hawkins/Bloomberg News/Landov; 6, © Kirsanov/Shutterstock; 7T, © Dana Milstead/iStockphoto; 7B, © Bilderbox/age fotostock; 9, © Christopher Badzioch/iStockphoto; 10, © James Robinson/Animals Animals Enterprises; 11, © James H. Robinson/Photo Researchers, Inc.; 12, © Lena Untidt/Bonnier Publications/Photo Researchers, Inc.; 13, © Mark Moffett/Minden Pictures; 14, © Dennis Whitehead/Corbis; 15, © Dr. Edward Ross/Visuals Unlimited/Corbis; 16, © Michael Maloney/San Francisco Chronicle/Corbis; 17, © Sinclair Stammers/Photo Researchers, Inc.; 18T, © Maria Zorn/Animals Animals Enterprises; 18B, © Kim Taylor/NPL/Minden Pictures; 19, © Dwight Kuhn/Dwight Kuhn Photography; 20, © John Mason/Ardea; 21T, © Kim Taylor/NPL/Minden Pictures; 21B, © Oxford Scientific/Photollibrary; 22, © Charles Melton/Visuals Unlimited/Getty Images; 23T, © Kenneth W. Fink/Photo Researchers, Inc.; 23B, © Donald Specker/Animals Animals Enterprises; 24, © age fotostock/SuperStock; 25, © Maryann Frazier/Photo Researchers, Inc.; 26, © Dan Ocampo/San Francisco Chronicle; 27, © age fotostock/SuperStock; 28, © Simon Smith/iStockphoto; 29T, © Premaphotos/Alamy; 29B, © Raymond Mendez/Animals Animals Enterprises; 31, © Dark Raptor/Shutterstock.

Publisher: Kenn Goin
Senior Editor: Lisa Wiseman
Creative Director: Spencer Brinker
Design: Dawn Beard Creative
Photo Researcher: Amy Dunleavy

Library of Congress Cataloging-in-Publication Data

Markovics, Joyce L.
    The honey bee's hive : a thriving city / by Joyce Markovics.
        p. cm. — (Spectacular animal towns)
    Includes bibliographical references and index.
    ISBN-13: 978-1-59716-867-0 (library binding)
    ISBN-10: 1-59716-867-X (library binding)
    1. Honeybee—Juvenile literature. I. Title. II. Title: Honeybee's hive.
    QL568.A6M523 2010
    595.79'9—dc22
                                            2009011295

For more information, write to Bearport Publishing Company, Inc., 101 Fifth Avenue, Suite 6R, New York, New York 10003. Printed in the United States of America in North Mankato, Minnesota.

032010
020810CG

10 9 8 7 6 5 4 3 2 1

Contents

Release the Honey Bees

California's almond trees were in full bloom in February 2006. Joe Traynor and his team stood under them ready to work. They had more than one million wooden boxes filled with 40 billion buzzing honey bees. Soon, the bees would zoom out of the boxes and begin their important work. In just 22 days, they would **pollinate** 600,000 acres (242,811 hectares) of almond trees!

An almond orchard in California

A honey bee

The buzzing sound that bees make is caused by their rapidly beating wings.

Joe used to be a beekeeper. Now, he works with almond growers to make sure they get enough bees to pollinate their trees at the right time. Through his work, Joe has been able to see firsthand how honey bees live.

After the flowers on an almond tree are pollinated, they will eventually shed their pink and white petals and turn into almonds, which are what the seeds of the fruit of the almond tree are called.

This beekeeper is unloading bees in an almond orchard in California.

Honey Bee Town

Honey bees are **insects** that live in **hives**. Just as many people live and work in a city, up to 50,000 honey bees live and work in a hive. This home is made up of a **honeycomb**, which bees build inside hollow trees, on tree branches, in holes in the ground, or in beekeepers' wooden boxes.

Beekeepers wear special clothing to protect themselves from stinging honey bees.

Due to a decreasing number of honey bees in the wild, more than half of the honey bees in the United States are raised by beekeepers. They are kept for the honey they make and their ability to pollinate the plants that people grow for food.

Honeycombs are built using beeswax that the insects make from special **glands** in their bodies. The bees chew the wax to shape it into thousands of tiny rooms called cells. These rooms are used in many different ways. For example, cells in the center of the hive hold baby bees. The outer rooms store food.

The cells in a honeycomb each have six sides.

Honey bees made this hive inside a beekeepers' wooden box.

Gathering Food Outside

Three kinds of bees live in a hive: workers, drones, and the queen. Each type of bee has a different job to help the **colony** live and grow. **Forager** bees are a kind of worker bee that helps the hive find food. They search for **pollen**, which they feed to their young. They also look for **nectar**, which they turn into honey.

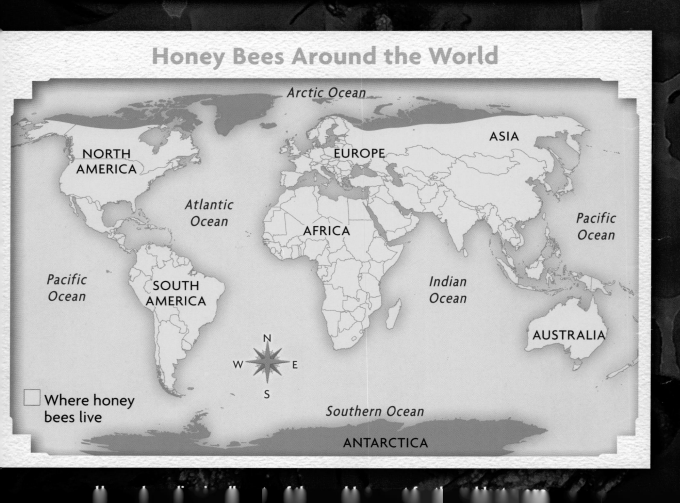

Honey Bees Around the World

Arctic Ocean

ASIA

NORTH AMERICA

EUROPE

Atlantic Ocean

AFRICA

Pacific Ocean

Pacific Ocean

SOUTH AMERICA

Indian Ocean

AUSTRALIA

N
W E
S

☐ Where honey bees live

Southern Ocean

ANTARCTICA

Just like many people, forager bees go to work in the morning. They dart from flower to flower, collecting food. Where do they store the food while they're working? The pollen that they gather is kept in the bees' long, curved hairs that form baskets on their hind legs. The nectar, which they suck from flowers using their hollow tongues, is stored in their stomachs. Once they have enough, the bees fly back to the hive.

This honey bee uses its tongue to drink nectar. The yellow ball on its leg is the pollen basket.

A forager bee flies up to two miles (3.2 km) away from the hive to find food. It may visit 10,000 flowers in one day!

Pollination

As forager bees gather food, they also help pollinate flowers. When a bee lands on a flower, pollen sticks to the hairs on its body. The bee then flies to another blossom, where some pollen on its body rubs off on the new flower's **stigma**, causing **fertilization**. Soon after, the flowers turn into seeds. These seeds will eventually fall off the plant and grow into new plants.

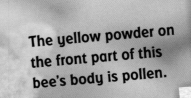

The yellow powder on the front part of this bee's body is pollen.

Honey bees help pollinate many types of plants. Apple and almond trees, blueberry bushes, and melon plants all rely on bees. Without bees, many of the fruits, vegetables, and nuts that humans like to eat could not be produced.

This pollen-covered honey bee is flying to another flower.

Honey bees pollinate around 130 types of crops in the United States—about one third of the food that people eat!

Dancing Bees

When forager bees find a great place for food, they fly back to their hive and tell the other bees. How? They dance!

There are two types of forager bee dances. The round dance lets other bees know that flowers are nearby—within 260 feet (79 m). The "tail-wagging" dance tells the bees that flowers are farther away. This dance also lets the bees know which direction to fly in order to find the flowers.

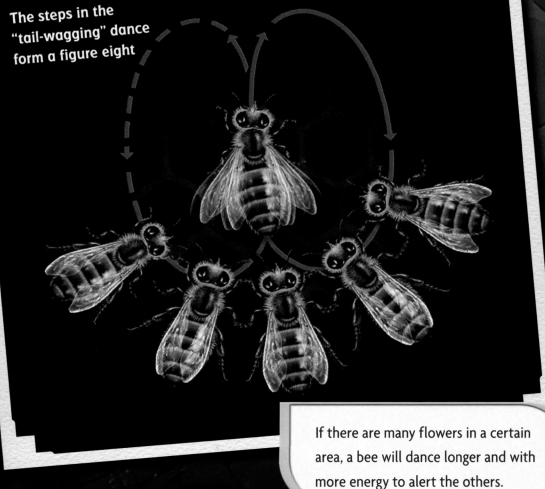

The steps in the "tail-wagging" dance form a figure eight

If there are many flowers in a certain area, a bee will dance longer and with more energy to alert the others.

Other forager bees watch these dances. When they get the information, they zip out of the hive to search for the flowers.

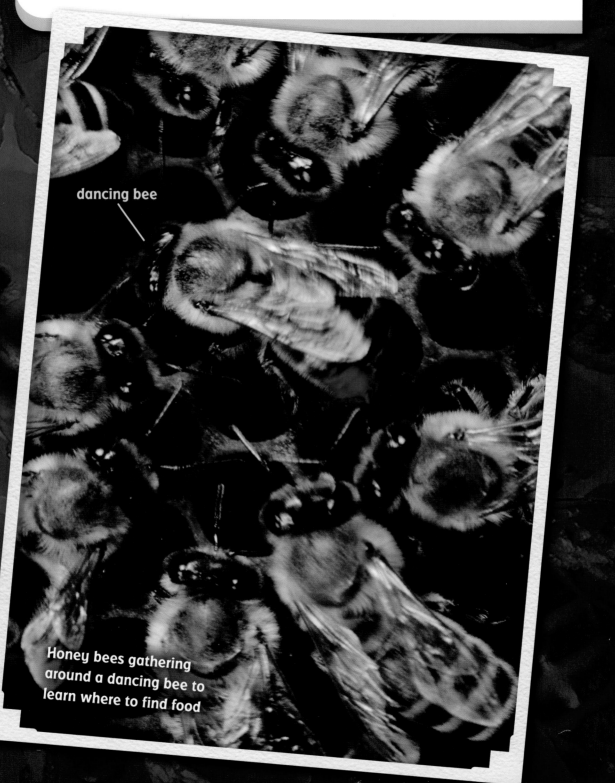

dancing bee

Honey bees gathering around a dancing bee to learn where to find food

Working on the Inside

The inside of a hive is like a busy city with many kinds of workers to help things run smoothly. Some workers help make food. They pack the pollen that forager bees have collected into honeycomb cells.

These bright yellow cells are filled with pollen.

Worker bees are also responsible for collecting nectar from forager bees. A forager bee spits the nectar into the mouth of a worker. Inside the worker's body, the nectar is mixed with chemicals. After 30 minutes, the worker bee spits the nectar into a cell and fans it with its wings. This helps the water from the nectar **evaporate**. A few hours later, the sweet liquid has turned into thick, gooey honey that's ready to eat.

In this photo, a forager bee passes nectar to another hive worker. The cells beneath them contain honey. During winter, one hive can eat up to 44 pounds (20 kg) of honey!

A colony also has other types of worker bees. "Guard" bees protect the hive from hungry animals such as bears. These bees will attack with their stingers. "House-cleaning" workers keep the hive tidy. They clean out used cells and remove dead bees.

Queen Bee

Some workers in the hive are in charge of caring for the most important bee—the queen. Each colony has only one. She produces chemicals called **pheromones** to communicate with the other bees. They smell the pheromones to find out what the queen wants them to do. For example, the queen's scent lets worker bees know when to feed, groom, and attend to her other needs.

This queen, the bee with the blue marker, is surrounded by workers.

The queen is larger than the other bees because she lays lots of eggs. In early summer, she **mates** only once with male bees, called **drones**, from other hives. The queen may mate with ten or more drones. After mating, the drones die. The queen, however, will go on to lay up to 1,500 eggs a day for the rest of her life. Most of the eggs will hatch into female worker bees. Some will hatch into drones, and a few will produce future queens.

A drone

All of the worker bees in a hive are females. Some hives have up to 50,000 workers. On the other hand, there are only about 500 to 1,000 drones in a hive. They live there but do no work.

A Town's Nursery

After a queen mates, she spends most of her life laying eggs. Each egg is laid in a **brood cell**. In three short days, the tiny eggs hatch into babies called **larvae**. Special worker bees, called nurse bees, care for the little insects.

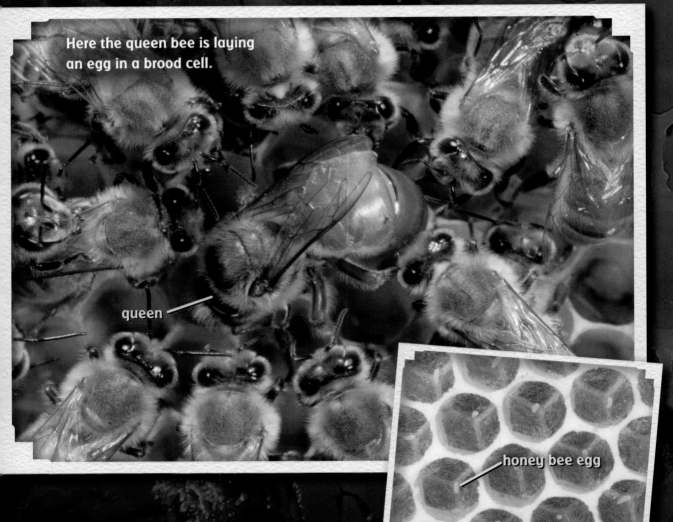

Here the queen bee is laying an egg in a brood cell.

queen

honey bee egg

Each honey bee egg is about half the size of a grain of rice.

The larvae will grow to about the size of a nickel in a week or so. For just a few days, the nurses feed the larvae a liquid they make called royal jelly, which is rich in the nutrients needed by the growing bees. Then the nurses feed the larvae "beebread" made from pollen and honey. Soon, the larvae are ready for a big change.

larvae

Bees use chemicals from their bodies to make nearly everything that they need, including wax and royal jelly.

New Members of the Colony

About nine days after the larvae hatch, nurses seal them into their brood cells using wax caps. Then the larvae spin a silk **cocoon** around themselves. At this stage, they are called **pupae**.

Inside their cells, the pupae undergo big changes. They grow wings and legs, and after a few weeks they become adult insects. This cycle of change is called **metamorphosis**.

These new adults eat their way out of their cells. Soon, they will start working in the hive. The youngest bees begin working inside the hive where it is safest. As they get older, they will work outside doing more dangerous jobs.

Developing pupae

Workers complete full metamorphosis in 21 days, while drones need 24 days.

The tiny black dots on the pupae's heads are simple eyes that can tell light from dark.

Outgrowing the Hive

Over time, a colony may become too big for its hive. Some members of a hive will then leave to start another one. These bees come together to form a **swarm**. The swarm sends out special scout bees to find a good place for a new hive. Once they find a spot, the bees start building the honeycomb.

A swarm of honey bees

Sometimes, a swarm of honey bees will take over another, smaller colony instead of forming a new one. The swarm will often kill the colony's queen.

If a queen moves to a new hive, worker bees from the old hive can make a new queen. To do this, they feed one female larva only royal jelly until she grows into an adult. This allows her to become a queen.

A swarm of honey bees building a honeycomb

These cells contain a developing queen.

Colony Collapse

Today, honey bees are facing a big problem—Colony Collapse Disorder, or CCD. Since 2006, some beekeepers have lost between 30 to 90 percent of their honey bees. What could be causing so many deaths? Scientists are not sure, but they have a few ideas.

A beekeeper checks to make sure a hive's larvae are healthy.

Pesticides might be one of the reasons for the huge loss of bees. Farmers spray these chemicals on plants to kill pests that eat their crops. Honey bees come into contact with these deadly chemicals when they search for food.

Mites may also be to blame. These tiny animals feed on bees' blood. Some scientists think that mites can transmit a virus that causes bees to get sick and die. Whatever the cause, the honey bees' future is at risk.

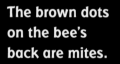

The brown dots on the bee's back are mites.

mites

A mite is a tiny spiderlike animal that has four pairs of legs and is related to a tick.

A Valuable Insect

In 2006, California's almond crop was huge—around one billion pounds (454 million kg)! After all the state's almond trees were pollinated, Joe Traynor could rest. Managing billions of bees is a big job. "You're really relieved when it's all over," says Joe. Like many others, however, he is worried about the bees' future.

Joe Traynor stands with some of his bees. Smoke from a can in Joe's hand helps to calm the bees.

He and other bee experts are working hard to help honey bees fight CCD. They are researching new ways to kill the mites. Scientists are also trying to keep farmers from using pesticides that could harm bees.

After all, honey bees are one of the world's most important insects. Not only do they live in spectacular animal towns, they also make honey and pollinate most of the plants that people grow for food.

People in the United States eat more than 400 million pounds (181 million kg) of honey each year.

Honey Bee Facts

Honey bees are social animals that live together in colonies. Here are some more facts about honey bees and their spectacular towns.

Size	workers: .4–.6 inches (10–15 mm) queens: .7–.9 inches (17–23 mm) drones: .6–.7 inches (15–17 mm)
Color	yellow and black
Food	honey, which is made from nectar, and pollen
Colony size	up to 50,000
Life Span	workers: 15–38 days queens: 3–5 years drones: about 90 days
Habitat	North America, South America, Africa, Europe, Asia, and Australia

More Animal Towns

Bees are not the only insects that live in spectacular towns. Here are two others.

Weaver ants

- Weaver ants live in colonies of up to 500,000 in tropical forests in Africa and Southeast Asia. They can also be found in Australia.
- They build nests in trees. A large colony of weaver ants might build many different nests in the same tree or in several trees.
- They use fresh leaves to build their nests. To do this, the ants line up and pull the edges of many leaves together. One ant then glues the leaf ends together using silk that ant larvae make.
- Weaver ants have a chemical in their bodies that can help fight some kinds of infections. People sometimes crush a few weaver ants to make medicine and then apply it to their skin.

Yellow jackets

- Yellow jackets are wasps with black and yellow stripes. They are about a half inch (13 mm) long and live in colonies.
- They eat insects such as flies, crickets, and caterpillars. They also like sweets and can be pests at picnics.
- These wasps have a painful sting. Unlike honey bees, yellow jackets can sting more than once without dying.
- They build round nests out of papery pulp that they make from trees. Yellow jackets build their nests in quiet, protected places. They may build their nests underground.

Glossary

brood cell (BROOD SEL) a tiny room in a hive used for breeding or raising young

cocoon (kuh-KOON) a covering that some insects make from silky threads

colony (KOL-uh-nee) a group of several thousand bees that work together to build nests, collect food, and raise young

drones (DROHNZ) male bees whose job it is to mate with the queen

evaporate (i-VAP-uh-rayt) to become less and then disappear

fertilization (*fur*-tuh-luh-ZAY-shuhn) the beginning stage of reproduction; for a flower, this happens when pollen comes into contact with a flower's stigma

forager (FOR-ij-ur) a bee or other animal that gathers food

glands (GLANDZ) body parts that produce natural chemicals

hives (HIVEZ) structures in which bees build honeycombs

honeycomb (HUHN-ee-kohm) a wax structure that bees make to store honey, pollen, and eggs

insects (IN-sekts) small animals that have six legs, three main body parts, two antennas, and a hard covering called an exoskeleton

larvae (LAR-vee) young insects at the stage of development between eggs and pupae

mates (MAYTS) comes together to have young

metamorphosis (*met*-uh-MOR-fuh-siss) the series of changes some animals go through when developing from eggs to adults

nectar (NEK-tur) a sweet liquid made by flowers that bees collect

pesticides (PESS-tuh-sidz) chemicals used to kill insects

pheromones (FAIR-uh-mohnz) chemicals, made by animals, used to send a message to other animals

pollen (POL-uhn) tiny yellow grains made by flowering plants

pollinate (POL-uh-nayt) to carry pollen from one flower to another, which fertilizes the second flower, allowing it to make seeds

pupae (PYOO-pee) young insects at the stage of development between larvae and adults

stigma (STIG-muh) the part of a flower that receives the pollen during pollination

swarm (SWORM) a group of bees clustered together

Bibliography

Bishop, Holley. *Robbing the Bees*. New York: Free Press (2005).

Jacobsen, Rowan. *Fruitless Fall*. New York: Bloomsbury (2008).

Mairson, Alan. "America's Beekeepers: Hive for Hire." *National Geographic* (May 1993).

honeybee.tamu.edu/

www.ars.usda.gov/News/docs.htm?docid=15572

www.sfgate.com/cgi-bin/article.cgi?f=/c/a/2007/10/14/CM2SS2SNO.DTL

Read More

Editors of Time for Kids. *Time for Kids: Bees!* New York: HarperCollins (2005).

Gibbons, Gale. *The Honey Makers*. New York: HarperCollins (2000).

Kalman, Bobbie. *The Life Cycle of a Honeybee*. New York: Crabtree Publishing Company (2004).

Milton, Joyce. *Honeybees*. New York: Grosset & Dunlap (2003).

Learn More Online

To learn more about honey bees and their colonies, visit
www.bearportpublishing.com/SpectacularAnimalTowns

Index

About the Author

Joyce L. Markovics is an editor, writer, and an insect lover.
She lives with her husband, Adam, who kindly tolerates
her fascination with six-legged creatures.